Trevor Wye
PRACTICE BOOK
for the Flute

Book 4

Intonation & Vibrato

Contents

Novello

For William Bennett – In Admiration

Published by
Novello Publishing Limited
14-15 Berners Street,
London W1T 3LJ, UK.

Exclusive Distributors:

Contact us:
Hal Leonard
7777 West Bluemound Road,
Milwaukee, WI 53213
Email: info@halleonard.com

In Europe, contact:
Hal Leonard Europe Limited
42 Wigmore Street, Marylebone,
London WIU 2RY
Email: info@halleonardeurope.com

In Australia, contact:
Hal Leonard Australia Pty. Ltd.
4 Lentara Court, Cheltenham,
Victoria 9132, Australia
Email: info@halleonard.com.au

Order No. NOV164153
ISBN 978-1-78305-422-0

Edited by Toby Knowles.
Music engraved by Paul Ewers Music Design.

Printed in the EU.

www.halleonard.com
www.wisemusicclassical.com

The Practice Book series is about effective practice: how to extract the most from it, how to be more skilled at it and how to isolate and overcome the problems and difficulties encountered in performing. It was written to help you achieve good results in the shortest time. If the advice is followed and the exercises practised properly, they will shorten the time taken to achieve success in the basics of flute playing and music making.

Practising

Practise because you want to. If you don't want to – don't. It is almost useless spending your practice time practising, but wishing that you weren't. Having decided to practise seriously, make it difficult. Examine all aspects of your tone, intonation and technique for flaws and practise to remove them. You will then make rapid progress. Practise what you can't play, or practise a technique you are not familiar with. Try not to indulge in too much self-flattery by playing through pieces or exercises you can already play well.

Many of these exercises are strenuous so be sure your posture and hand positions are correct. Consult a good teacher or if you are in doubt, refer to *Practice Book 6 – Advanced Practice* (NOV164175) or look at *Efficient Practice* (Trevor Wye; Falls House Press), or *Proper Flute Playing* (NOV120651), the companion book to the *Practice Book* series, which contains a guide on how best to schedule these exercises.

How to make the best use of your practice time

Most of us have a limit on how much time we have to practise. Let's assume that the four subjects below are the priority. Each should take up about one quarter of your total technical practice time, though this can be varied according to needs:

Tone • Expression and Intonation • Technique • Scales and Arpeggios

Of course you will have other subjects to work on too, but this is a scheme which will help most people. Technique (finger independence) is not quite the same as scales and arpeggios, which are the building blocks of musical composition.

Articulation needs extra time, though if your articulation is good, you can incorporate this into Scales and Technique sessions by varying the articulation patterns as shown in *Practice Book 2 – Technique* (NOV164131) and *Practice Book 5 – Breathing & Scales* (NOV164164). *Practice Book 3 – Articulation* (NOV164142) suggests ways to achieve clear and rapid tonguing effectively.

GUARANTEE

Possession of this book is no guarantee that you will improve on the flute; there is no magic in the printed paper. But, if you have the desire to play well and if you put in some diligent practice, you cannot fail to improve. It is simply a question of *time*, *patience* and *intelligent* work. The book is designed to avoid unnecessary practice. It is concentrated stuff. Provided that you follow the instructions carefully, you should make more than twice the improvement in half the time!

That is the guarantee.

This is one of a series of six books for players of all ages who have been learning the flute from about a year upwards and including those at college or university. The material has been spread out over the six books and should be selected and practised as needed. The speed of the exercises should be chosen to accommodate the skill and age of the player. Some exercises are more difficult than others. Simply use those that are the most useful.

The other books in this series are:

PRACTICE BOOK for the Flute

These books were revised and updated in 2013/2014.
© Trevor Wye

A Plan For Using This Book

Step One   Read this book carefully and slowly and take time to fully understand what it is about. It is not easy to understand for those who are unfamiliar with science.
If the science is too much for you, at least read the section, 'The Flute Scale' on p.15.

Step Two   Hopefully you will also have a copy of *Practice Book 1*. Practise the the Pitch Control; Endings and Nuance; Flexibility Exercises in *Practice Book 1*.

Step Three   Practise the 24 Studies in this book when you have completed the other steps above.

Finally
Play slow tunes using a lot of dynamic variation.

FOREWORD

This Practice Book relates to everything concerned with playing in tune and follows on from *Practice Book 1 – Tone*, which deals with the basics of pitch control. This book takes you further: you will discover the reasons why we have to alter notes in a chord, especially when in an ensemble or orchestra, in order to play properly in tune. The scientific material may be difficult to understand, therefore a big effort has been made to explain it in simple language using terms that are easy to understand. Take time to read the text and in due course it will become clearer.

Just reading through the book will not give you the ability to play in tune: the exercises should be practised carefully and often. The acquisition of a good 'ear' does not come easily, and even when obtained, needs frequent refreshment. Without regular practice, the ability to hear small changes in pitch, and hear faults in intervals can soon be lost. Piano tuners, after a holiday, have to sharpen up their ears before starting work again. Teachers, who may often be listening to the poor intonation of beginners, will need to take special care when practising. The daily exposure to poor intonation is damaging in the short term. Their ears will need to be 'sharpened' up when practising.

To get the most out of this book, you will need a few tools: an electronic tuning device; a well-tuned piano; some basic adjusting tools for your flute such as a good screwdriver – but most of all *time, patience*, and *intelligent work*.

If you suspect your flute may not be tuned to a modern scale, first turn to the section headed 'The Flute Scale' and read it carefully. Then turn back to the section headed 'The Chord of Nature'. Be sure to check that you have worked at *Practice Book 1*, specifically the section called 'Pitch Control'. That will provide the basics for working at the exercises in this book. There are some interesting experiments to be tried and even some Trios for two flutes!

THE CHORD OF NATURE

For this first experiment you will need a piano which is well in tune. It is not important, at this stage, if the piano is above or below pitch though it must be in tune with itself. First, open the lid wide. If it is an upright piano, remove the top front. The fasteners for this can be found just inside the top lid on the left and right. Find a bass note on the piano which is rich, vibrant and in tune – some notes have two or three strings each – it is important that the note has no sourness. Play the note *forte* and see if you can hear more than one note sounding softly above your chosen note. With practice, you will soon hear eight or even ten different notes sounding together above your chosen bass note. To help you hear these notes more easily, play the bass note (in the example below, it is F) with one hand, and with the other strike the octave above, briefly:

You should hear the octave sounding together with the bass note. The short note doesn't make the upper note sound; it simply draws your attention to the note you should listen for. Now continue with the exercise below. Allow about ten seconds for each held bass note as some of the upper notes become apparent only after a few seconds have elapsed. *Do not use the pedal.*

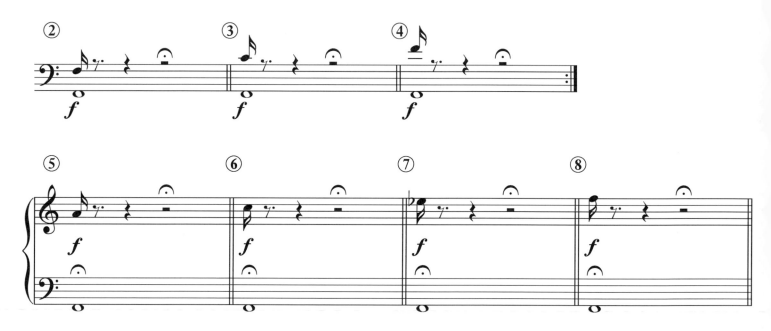

By now you will have heard most, if not all, of the upper notes. These are called harmonics or overtones and have a specific relationship to the bass note or fundamental. If you have some difficulty in hearing any of these notes, move your head a little.

Now for another experiment; after listening to all the harmonics, hold down the sustaining pedal, and sound your low note again. You will clearly hear all the harmonics sounding as a rich chord, rather like an organ:

For the next experiment, without holding down the sustaining pedal, you must push down the key for one of the short notes, or harmonics, without the hammer hitting the string and causing the note to sound, and then strike your bass note again loudly. After about a second, release the bass note. Listen.

Repeat for all eight 'harmonic' notes separately. Taking the damper off the upper note allows it to sound in sympathy with the harmonics of the bass note. This is called 'sympathetic vibration'. Some sympathetic notes sound rather louder than others. To experience more sympathetic vibration, hold down the sustaining pedal and sing a note loudly into the piano.

Now try different vowel sounds: Oooh, Aaah, Eeeh etc. Notice that the piano 'plays back' the original sound. This is because each vowel sound has a different mixture of harmonics. **Remember that the harmonics never change their sequence**: what makes the sounds alter is the relative strength of each of the harmonics in the vowel sound. The understanding of this fact is important to any study of tone or intonation because the fundamental tone of all musical instruments is exactly alike; the reason why we hear differences between say, a flute and an oboe is because the flute has few harmonics sounding with any note (about five) and an oboe has many (about thirteen)*. Why do we hear a difference between two different flute players? Because the sound each player makes – though playing the same notes with the same harmonics – contains different quantities of each harmonic. If flour is the basic ingredient of a cake, then varying the quantity of fruit, eggs, sugar and butter will produce different cakes, though the ingredients remain the same. Try the piano experiment with a different piano and you will have less difficulty in hearing some harmonics and more difficulty in hearing others, especially the seventh harmonic. Piano makers deliberately try to suppress the seventh harmonic because it sounds so out of tune with the natural note on the piano:

Once again play your bass note:

Fix your ear, after a few seconds, on to the seventh harmonic. Now softly play the minor seventh on the piano:

There is a slight but discernible difference in intonation between the notes. Which is right? They both are! The natural note has been tuned (or adjusted) to conform with Equal Temperament without which it would be impossible to play in all keys. More of this later in the section headed **Scales**.

* *The starting transient is the scientific term to describe the first fraction of a second of a note and is the other determining factor which helps us recognise different musical sounds.*

Here is a list of the Harmonic Series up to the eighth harmonic. There are, of course, many more beyond the first eight, but this list will serve us for now.

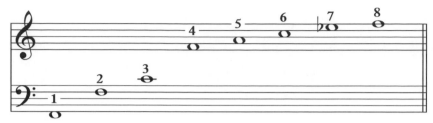

**Fundamental
or 1st harmonic**

Another harmonic which does not agree with Equal Temperament to which your piano is tuned is the fifth harmonic (A, if you are using F as your bass note). When your bass note has been sounded, the fifth harmonic (which gives, in effect, a major third) rings out loud and clear. What, then, if you wish to play the chord of F *minor* using your bass F as the root of this chord? A♭ is going to clash badly with the fifth harmonic which is A natural. Play the chord of F major, later adding an A♭ softly at the pitch of the fifth harmonic. *Ouch!* So thought the ancient musicians who decided that any minor chord which has to be sustained for any length became painful, and was better changed to a major chord – especially at the end of a piece – so as to avoid the minor third clashing with the fifth harmonic. This effect is otherwise known as the *Tierce De Picardie*.

Do all minor chords have to be changed to major chords? No, they just have to be better in tune to sound right, although if you now play alternate major and minor chords on the piano, you will hear a clarity about the major chord and a bit of *ouch!* in the minor. The scoring of the chord is important, of course, and a well-scored chord can sound 'cleaner'. The pitch of any note can also be changed very slightly on the piano by playing each note with a different nuance: loud = sharper; soft = flatter. A dominant seventh chord will sound better when the seventh is played softly. Although no flute playing has taken place yet – don't worry! A clear understanding of what has gone before and what is to follow is vital to any future intonation practice.

SCALES

No, not the sort you have to practise to acquire a technique, but the division of the octave into notes and intervals. Music making came first: constructing scales came later to meet the needs of music. In the earliest European music, the need to change key often, as we do today, was not required by composers or listeners. Chord changes were simple. Music was based on the intervals in the Chord of Nature, or the natural Harmonic Series, which means that the notes of the scale match the Harmonic Series you have heard. Unfortunately, the distance between each semitone is not the same. The octave is divided into twelve slightly unequal parts. The notes in this scale when played as chords are pleasing to the ear but if any note of this scale is used as the tonic of a new scale, the notes in the new key wouldn't correspond with the notes of the old key. In other words, as the music changed into more remote keys, it would sound less and less pleasing. If one wants to modulate into other keys, the best compromise is to divide the octave into twelve equal parts: the Equal Tempered Scale.

Here (on the facing page) is a diagram which shows the difference between an Equal Tempered Scale and Just Scale or a scale according to the harmonic series.

EQUAL TEMPERED SCALE

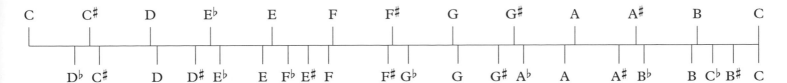

JUST SCALE

Take a ruler and imagine 0 as C natural; 1cm as C♯; 2cm as D; 3cm as E♭, 4cm as E natural, etc. The interval C-E, a major third, would appear on the Just Scale as about 3.75 cm. Suppose we wanted to use the E (3.75cm) as the starting point to measure another interval. The measurements would not coincide with the remaining measured marks. To change key from C Major to E Major would mean using 3.75cm as the starting point. To put it another way, **imagine a ruler exactly 12cm long on which the distance between each centimetre varied!**

The only sensible solution to our dilemma is to divide the ruler into exactly equal parts, then any point on the ruler can be used as a new starting point. This is the same with the octave, which is divided into twelve equal parts, giving us Equal Temperament.

The advantages of Equal Temperament are:

1. Changing key, even to remote keys, sounds pleasing on any instrument.
2. All instruments will match each other in scale and enable them to play together.

The disadvantage is that there is a small but discernible 'out of tuneness' in some intervals particularly major and minor thirds. Look as the diagram again. On the Just Scale there is a difference between F♯ and G♭. Though these are not shown on the diagram, there are also different positions for both double sharps and double flats. To play on a flute constructed to a Just Scale and be able freely to change key, you would need thirty-five notes to one octave and a lot more fingers and arms to play it! As it is, without double sharps and flats, there are twenty notes as compared with twelve notes in the Equal Temperament scale.

In other sections in this book, you will be making experiments to allow you to hear these Just Intonation intervals and to appreciate them, although it is not the purpose here to return to the past. Equal Temperament is most certainly here to stay. We have all had our ears trained to hear Equal Temperament as *in tune* when, in fact, it isn't! One writer referred to it as the Equal *Tampered* Scale.

If everyone were to play exactly in tune with Equal Temperament however, it would sound very pleasing to the ear, or, acceptably out of tune! When you have fully understood the next section, you will have a clear idea in which direction to move when you are out of tune with another instrument. Playing in tune will follow. It is a question of a 'good ear' plus ...., ..., and .... !

FLUTE HARMONICS

Now take up your flute and play low C, overblowing it until it plays the octave above (the same exercise as in *Practice Book 1 – Tone*).

2nd harmonic

The octaves *should* be in tune (but see the section headed **The Flute Scale**).

Now overblow C until it produces G.

3rd harmonic

Quickly compare the pitch with the natural G fingering.

compare

There is a change in quality – ignore this. Listen only to the pitch. There should only be a very slight difference in pitch.

Overblow now to the fourth and on to the fifth harmonic – E above the stave. Compare the pitch of the harmonic E with your natural E fingering. You will notice a large difference: the harmonic E is considerably flatter and will correspond in pitch with the E natural in the diagram of the two Temperaments. Continue the series – if you can – to the sixth harmonic – G – and on to the seventh. When comparing this B♭ with the usual fingering, it seems to be neither B♭ nor A, but somewhere in between. It corresponds with A♯ in the diagram on the Just Scale.

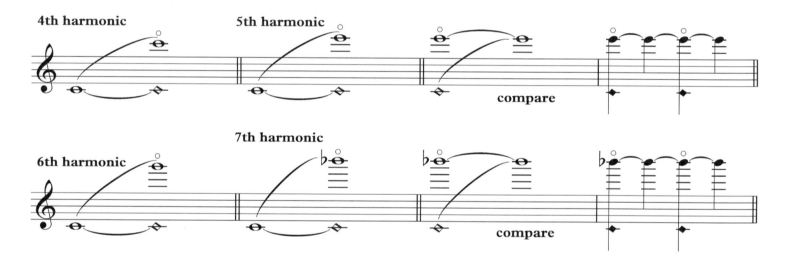

4th harmonic **5th harmonic** compare

6th harmonic **7th harmonic** compare

Having observed these differences in pitch between the harmonics and the Equal Tempered tuning on your flute, where does this lead us? Musical scales are made in the process of trying to make music.

It is obvious that to play in all keys at pleasure, the distance between each semitone must be the same. This idea of dividing the octave into twelve equal parts is not new; it was first put forward by the Chinese about five thousand years ago and championed by many composers of the 18th century including J. S. Bach.

To repeat once more: Equal Temperament means having exactly the same distance between semitones and that, in turn, means division of the octave into twelve equal semitones. Look at the table on the next page: for simplicity, you will see listed the C Major scale but including an E♭ so that you can compare the C Major and C Minor scales.

A semitone can be divided up into one hundred parts and each part called a cent. There are 1200 cents to the octave. In the left hand column are the diatonic intervals from C. Next, are the same notes in cents. The next column contains the intervals in a Just Scale, also divided into cents.

The adjustments you might make to play properly in tune are shown in the right hand column headed **Result**. The amount of sharpness or flatness required to play in tune is measured in 'OGGS'. It's just a made-up word to describe a pitch difference. For example, if you are playing from C up to E, the E should be flattened by seven OGGS – or quite a lot! – in order to make the major third sound in tune.

The interval C-G (a 'perfect fifth') is very slightly sharper than in Equal Temperament: it is sharper by one ogg, the smallest 'ogg' interval! It could be translated as 'a tiny bit'.

NOTE	EQUAL TEMPERAMENT in Cents	JUST TEMPERAMENT in Cents	RESULT THE DIFFERENCE in Oggs
C	0	0	0
D	200	204	+2
E♭	300	316	+8
E	400	386	-7
F	500	498	-1
G	700	702	+1
A	900	884	-8
B	1100	1088	-6
C	1200	1200	0

If you really want to sound in tune, you will constantly have to adjust your intonation, depending:
a) on which key you are in, and b) on the other instruments playing with you.

I must repeat once again: **This book does not set out to suggest that you must play according to a Just Temperament scale.** What you learn from it is that if you have the E natural in the chord of C Major it will sound acceptable if it is in accordance with equal temperament. It will be unacceptably out of tune if it is sharper than equal temperament. It will sound perfectly in tune (provided all the other instruments are in tune) if it is flattened by 7 oggs below equal temperament.

The chart needs now to be translated into intervals in all keys rather than just in C Major and the adjustment you might wish to make committed to memory:

INTERVAL	ADJUSTMENT IN OGGS
MAJOR SECOND	+2
MINOR THIRD	+8
MAJOR THIRD	-7
PERFECT FOURTH	-1
PERFECT FIFTH	+1
MAJOR SIXTH	-8
MAJOR SEVENTH	-6

Notice that if the interval of a perfect fifth has to be made bigger by 1 ogg, the remainder of the octave – a perfect fourth – also has to be reduced by 1 ogg or the two intervals won't fit in to an octave! The same is the case with a minor third (+8 oggs) and a major third (-7 oggs), to fit into a perfect fifth. The intervals have to be adjusted. To sum up: read this section again if you are not sure of it. Playing in tune means being able to adjust in the right direction according to the pitch of the other players or the surrounding notes. You are not taking a step back into the past. Equal Temperament is here to stay. Clear recognition of Just Temperament enables you to play in Equal Temperament or to make slight adjustments according to the circumstances in order to play better than Equal Temperament. Put another way, it will help you to play really in tune.

Finally, the adjustment to the intonation refers to the key you are in. When the piece changes key, the adjustments change, though you will probably not get as far as that stage. It will be found sufficient to appreciate the necessary adjustments in the key in which you are playing.

The following piece is a good example of changing intonation. The changes are only small. The asterisks indicate the notes you should be most conscious of. As the piano part is largely arpeggios it is not so important to play each flute note at the same pitch as the piano. If, however, the piano part has block chords – as illustrated for simplicity in the example below – then playing each note at the same pitch as the piano would be necessary. You will have to use your judgement as to when it sounds more beautiful to play out of tune with the piano!

MADRIGAL

P. GAUBERT

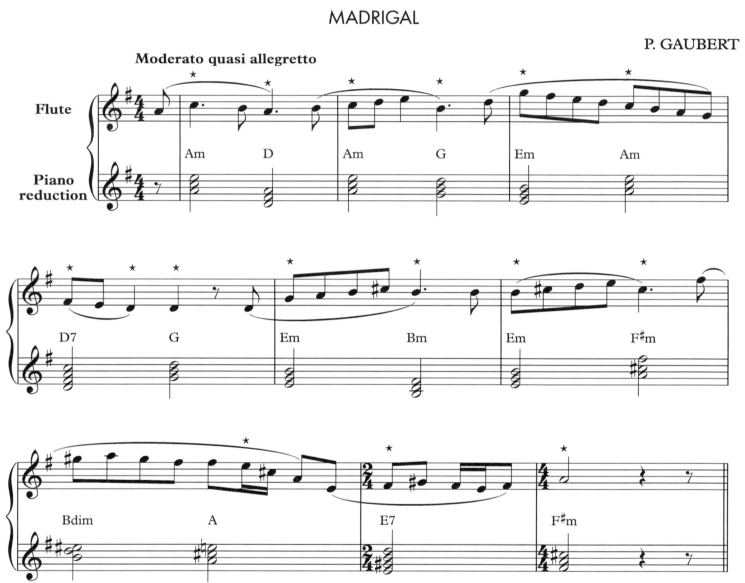

The final chord of the whole piece is G major of which the flute has a B, the major third.
Ask your pianist to omit the B in the right hand and play your B flatter by 7 oggs.

DIFFERENCE TONES

Now for the proof, using your flute. For this next experiment you will need another flute player. The two flutes should be played without vibrato or any kind of wobble. Tune the two flutes perfectly to the upper D (two octaves above middle C) played *forte*. Whilst player one is holding his D, player two should play B♭ below it. Immediately an uncomfortable buzz will be heard, the result of interaction between the two notes. This buzz will, on careful listening, be apparent as a noticeably flat B sounding nearly two octaves below. It is a Difference Tone. It is called a Difference Tone because it is a note which sounds as a result of hearing two simultaneous clear tones; it is the mathematical difference of frequency between the two notes.

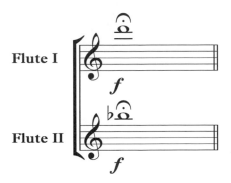

Flute I

Flute II

At concert pitch (A=440 Hz.), the pitch of the two notes is:

D=1174.6 Hz. (cycles per second)
B♭=932.3 Hz.

Subtract one from the other, the difference being 242.3 Hz. which is a little flatter than a B natural two octaves below. (B natural is 246.9 Hz.). If you like a chord of B natural + B♭ + D then I won't intervene! Most people don't, so reduce the size of the major third either by sharpening the B♭ or flattening D until the difference tone becomes B♭ exactly two octaves below the B♭ played by the second flute. The chord will then sound in tune.

Notice that raising the lower note or flattening the higher note of any interval flattens the Difference Tone. Now for another three-part chord played by two flutes:

1st flute plays high D again and
2nd flute plays B natural below it.

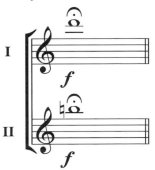

I

II

The result is a minor third. But another note way below can be heard. Subtract B from D.

D = 1174.6 Hz.
B = 987.8 Hz.

186.8 Hz.

This gives a difference tone of 186.8 which is very close to F♯ in the low register. What we need to do to make the two notes sound sweet and in tune is to make the F♯ Difference Tone rise to a G natural. To make the difference tone rise, the interval has to be made larger. Therefore, the 2nd flute, who plays the B natural, must flatten it with his lips until the Difference Tone – F♯ – rises to G natural, giving a perfect triad of G Major.

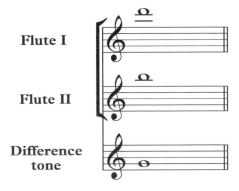

Flute I

Flute II

Difference tone

To reinforce this point, all intervals produce Difference Tones which can only clearly be heard when the instruments playing them have few, if any, natural harmonics in the tone. Two oboes would be useless for this experiment as they have many natural harmonics sounding with the fundamental. Two flutes are ideal. **13**

To further illustrate Difference Tones, here are three trios for two flutes! Careful examination of the chart on page 11 and a careful adjustment of the requisite oggs will produce the bass line illustrated in the first two trios. Memorise the Oggs Chart and use your ears. It is better for one player only to make these adjustments.

TRIOS FOR TWO FLUTES

ARBEAU–WARLOCK

GOD SAVE THE QUEEN

In this 'trio' below the tune appears in the Difference Tones. What is the tune?

Try writing your own trio for two flutes! Have you been wondering why equal temperament tuning hasn't worried you, or others before you? It has, though music has become so harmonically complex that the differences don't show as much as in earlier, purer music. Seventy years ago a lecturer on music said, 'The human ear is much like the back of a donkey; you can whip it into callousness to almost any kind of harmonic punishment.' How very true that is today!

THE FLUTE SCALE

Before going further, an examination should be made of the scale of your flute. Since the 1980s, flute makers have re-examined the 'scale' of the flute, that is to say, the positioning of the tone holes so that you, the player can more easily play in tune.

As equal temperament is the measure by which we calculate the correct placing of the tone holes to provide a perfect scale, there should be no problem. Unfortunately, not all makers agree with each other about this. Each maker seems to have their own scale. That makes it difficult for us, the players, to know what we should do to play in tune.

When Boehm designed the modern flute in 1847 he developed a precise method of calculating the position of the tone holes and hence, the intonation. The pitch in use at this time was A=435 Hz. (meaning 435 cycles per second). Gradually, between 1847 and 1930, the pitch generally in use rose to A=440 Hz. Though the flute makers made adjustments to the scale, such as moving the A natural hole closer to the mouth hole, a rise in pitch would require all the tone holes to be moved. Each manufacturer found his own method of doing this and not until fairly recently did any re-examination of the complete scale take place, largely due to the work of Albert Cooper of London. He devised a scale which lowered the traditionally sharp notes in the left hand (C♯ and C natural, etc.) and raised the flat notes at the lower end of the flute. The result is Cooper's Scale, a scheme for the size and position of the tone holes to enable us to play an Equal Tempered scale without having to make big adjustments with the lips. It is enough to have to do battle with draughty halls, differently pitched pianos, the temperature of the room, and the problems of other players, without having the added problem of one's own flute.

A modern scale flute such as Cooper's will not solve all problems. Adjustments will still have to be made in different performing conditions. In general, a traditional scale flute is sharp on some left hand notes and flat in the right hand lower notes, or expressed another way: the octave length of the flute is too long. Check your flute's tuning yourself. First, tune carefully to a tuning fork, then play low C followed by the first harmonic of C. Then slur to the natural left hand fingering of C:

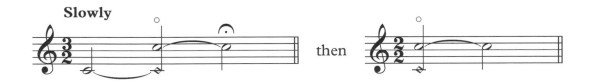

There is a change of tone quality but the notes should be in tune. **Make no attempt to tune the notes with your lips**.

Repeat with C♯:

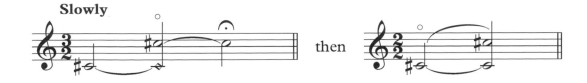

Do the upper Cs and C♯s appear to be sharper than the harmonics? They shouldn't be. If they are, the chances are that your flute is a traditional scale flute. But first, some further checks. If you've already read the section headed **The Chord Of Nature** you will realise that a perfect fifth is a near perfect interval in Equal Temperament. Therefore, also check the fifths:

Be sure not to move your lips in an attempt to tune the notes. The normal fingering should sound very slightly flat (1 ogg!).

Most flutes seem to have a sharp C♯ and the amount of sharpness varies from maker to maker. Some more recent flutes have other problems such as a sharp C♯, and a flat B natural; a flat B♭ and a flat footjoint, the latter making the lowest notes too flat and difficult to play in tune when playing ***pp***. Some makers have moved on from Cooper's Scale – which is very good and causes no serious problems – to Bennett's Scale, an improved scale*. It might be advisable to ask your dealer which scale your potential purchase is made to.

Flutes are made to different pitches too, and we can buy flutes at A=440; A=442 and A=444 and even sharper ones. It is important to understand that a flute can only be made to perform perfectly at one pitch. Moving the headjoint in or out is a stopgap measure and if the flute has a flatter scale than the pitch at which you want to perform, a lot of lip adjustment has to be made, which can be exhausting. Even with a modern and well tuned flute, you may still wish to adjust the pitch of a note slightly.

Study the diagram below. The names of the tone holes are not always the same as you may have thought. We commonly refer to the tone hole names by the name of the note produced by the finger placed over them.

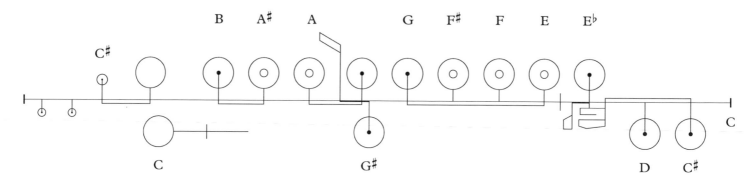

To make some adjustment to your flute, you will need some plasticine or play-doh and a toothpick or a sharpened matchstick. To adjust the C♯, remove the left-hand C♯ rod with a small screwdriver. It is a long rod and will release the left hand keys, though don't take those off: just remove the C♯ key. Clean out the tone hole with a cloth and then roll a piece of plasticine between your finger and thumb and wipe it against the edge of the tone hole as shown below.

HEAD JOINT ←   → FOOT JOINT

* *William Bennett is the dedicatee of this book: his intonation when performing is without parallel. He has experimented, together with Cooper, to produce a good reliable scale (known as R.S. 2012) which has been taken up by one large Japanese flute maker and several smaller USA makers. If the performer has serious problems on these flutes, the fault probably lies with the player.*

By doing this the vibrating column of air will have further to travel down the tube before escaping and so the note will be flatter. Sculpt the plasticine carefully with a toothpick and remove any from the top of the tone hole so that on replacing the key, the pad will not come into contact with it. Replace the mechanism. Try the tuning exercise again. If further adjustments are needed, add or subtract more plasticine.

These adjustments to the tuning will not affect the tone to any discernible degree. Don't worry about lumps appearing in the bore of the flute. Do not swab out your flute. When satisfied, play it for a week. Then, replace the plasticine (some of which may have fallen out anyway) with a fibreglass paste or a car body repair paste, widely available. This substance can be scraped or filed away to fine-tune the note. It can also, if required, easily be removed by exerting pressure on it when dried. This technique has a twofold effect on the scale: it causes the air column to travel farther and it makes the hole smaller, both of which flatten a note.

Some further checks:

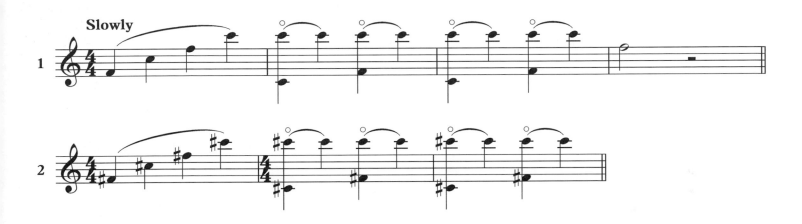

It is quite impossible to say what should be done to your flute. Each maker has a different scale. Generally speaking, however, traditional scale flutes have a very sharp C♯ and C natural and a quite sharp A♯ in the left hand. Only F♯ is often sharp in the right hand. From F natural down, the notes get progressively flatter.

N.B. Be sure the cork in the headjoint is correctly placed. It should be 17.3mm from the centre of the embouchure hole. Most cleaning sticks have a line engraved at this point which should appear in the centre of the embouchure hole. It should never be moved from this position as it affects the TONE throughout the entire compass and the intonation of the third octave from D upwards. The point of this section is, then, to flatten any sharp notes. Flat notes can't be sharpened, but flattening the sharp notes and pushing the head joint further in, will sharpen all the notes. If necessary, half a centimetre could be cut off the socket end of the headjoint to enable the head to be pushed in more, though do take note of the last two paragraphs of the section headed **Tuning Up**.

PERFECT PITCH

Many players claim to have *perfect pitch*. Perfect or absolute pitch is the ability to identify a musical sound accurately without the help of a reference sound. This ability is rare. The ability to identify a note by comparison with a remembered note is common and can be acquired with a little effort. This is called *relative pitch*. Carry a tuning fork around and practise comparing everyday sounds with it. For a few months listen to the tuning fork before going to sleep. After some practice, you will recall the pitch of the fork at any time.

TUNING UP

Musical performances are often spoiled by the inability of the young student to tune correctly. Look at these portraits to see if you can recognise yourself:

The player and pianist walk on to the platform. The pianist plays an A which is a signal for the flute player to blot out the note he has heard by performing a few short rapid scales or loud random notes. He makes no adjustment to the flute. He coughs. He adjusts his music and his tie, and starts to play.

This is the timid one: he plays a *staccatissimo*, *pianissimo* A, peers down the flute like a telescope, as if he is Vasco da Gama sighting land, nods confidently to the pianist and begins.

As above, only this is a more experienced player; he has observed what professional players do at recitals and he imitates their method of warming up. Offstage can be heard the final variation of the 'Carnival of Tunis'; the audience waits expectantly. He walks on; the pianist plays an A, which the flautist disdains; it must be the wrong flavour! He minutely examines a part of the mechanism and nods to the pianist. It's very impressive until he begins the first phrase.

The whole object of tuning up is to tune up! No player, however advanced, can hope to give a good performance and give pleasure to his audience without first establishing a pitch relationship with the other player or players. Most often the performer cannot hear the pitch easily and, feeling that he ought to be able to, tries to cover his inadequacy. Allow me to let you into a secret: *tuning up with any instrument, particularly the piano, is not easy*. You are not the only one!

Now to practicalities:

How is the tuning best done? Assuming that the section in the front of this book has been carefully read, tuning up becomes easier with a little practice. You must start from the position of not knowing whether you are sharp, flat, or in tune. Don't try to understand too quickly or you will not understand at all. The problem is to compare, assess and adjust with the pitch of another instrument.

> *'If I don't know I don't know,*
> *I think I know.*
> *If I don't know I know,*
> *I think I don't know.'*

KNOTS R. D. Laing
(reprinted by permission Tavistock Publications Ltd)

Try it this way using the upper A:

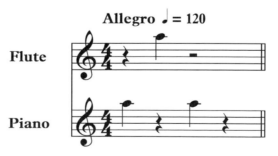

Make a judgement: are you sharper, flatter, or the same as the two outside notes? If in doubt, guess. Then adjust and repeat. Again, make a judgement. Don't wait. Make an immediate judgement, right or wrong. Then, adjust accordingly and repeat. Do this until you are satisfied. Make certain you are playing with the same sound as when playing your solo. If, during the piece, you feel that the pitch is still not correct, then re-adjust during some bars' rest or at the end of the movement. A slow, quiet movement may sound slightly flatter than you would wish; before playing slow movements, push the head in a little, though do remember to pull the head out again for the last movement. Don't be ashamed or embarrassed about tuning up in public. Take your time.

For the flute, the note A natural is not a very satisfactory note to tune to. You will get a better idea of the total tuning by repeating the above with middle D instead of A. Be in no doubt as to what happens when the headjoint is pushed in:

Suppose you tune to C natural in the left hand, and, sounding flat, you push the head in by 1cm to sharpen it. The distance from the mouth hole to the C natural hole is about 27cm. You have, therefore, shortened the distance to C by 1/27th. The lower C – an octave lower – which has a tube length of about 60cm has been shortened by 1/60th. As 1/27th is the greater fraction, the upper C will have been sharpened by roughly twice the amount of the lower C.

When tuning, therefore, it is wise to tune both A and D, lest when pulling out for A, the D becomes too flat. This underlines the point that a flute can ideally only be constructed to be played at one pitch. One could go further and say that it can only be played at one pitch, by one player at one temperature. Anything else is a compromise. Therefore, D would be a more practical note to tune to after checking A.

VIBRATO

Vibrato is a fluctuation in the flute tone, about three quarters of which is a rise and fall in pitch, while the remainder is a rise and fall in volume or loudness. Read through this section first to see what it entails.

It has been said that vibrato is something a performer should feel, not something to be learned. For those who feel it – and produce vibrato naturally – this may be true. For the large majority who can't do it and want to know how to do it, it is something that should be studied and correctly learnt. String players study vibrato in great detail. Vibrato has only been in universal use during the last two centuries. In the 18th century it was used on some long notes as an ornament. During the early part of the 19th century, vibrato was used to mark the high points in a phrase. With the wide acceptance of the Boehm flute, its use increased though each country developed its own vibrato style. In the advent of Impressionism, it was more widely used and has now become part of the normal colouring of flute tone.

If you were to study the vibrato of singers and players you would notice that vibrato rarely goes above seven wobbles and rarely below four wobbles per second. It is desirable to vary the vibrato according to the mood and the speed of the music, and the octave in which one is playing.

The exercises which follow will train you in the use of vibrato between 4 and 7 wobbles per second. There are three basic ways of producing a fluctuation in pitch:

a.   by moving the lips or jaw by alternately compressing and relaxing the lips
b.   by opening and shutting the throat
c.   by using the larynx
d.   by fluctuating the air speed and therefore the air pressure with the diaphragm

Techniques (c) and (d) are jointly the most commonly used method, which is recommended because:

i.   it allows the lips solely to perform the function of forming the embouchure
ii.   it allows the throat to remain open and relaxed – probably the most important single factor in tone production
iii.   it encourages the correct use of the diaphragm for tonal support. Vibrato is a regular equal rise and fall in the pitch of a note. Rise and fall. If the vibrato only rises above the note, the ear hears the average or mean pitch which would be sharper. Remember that the flute was once played without vibrato. The production of a clear straight tone is essential before adding any wobble.

STAGE ONE

Play a few long notes without any fluctuation in pitch. Use the abdominal muscles as in sighing. If any involuntary, unwanted vibrato is already being produced, try to eliminate it or see the Problem Box at the end of this section. When your tone is straight, play a low G, holding the flute only with the left hand. Place your right hand on your abdomen and push and relax your right hand alternately rhythmically to achieve an increase and decrease in air speed. Start at about two or three wobbles per second. It is similar to silently saying 'ha, ha, ha, ha'. See the diagram below.

When this is working, try to achieve the same result with the abdominal muscles only, holding the flute with both hands. The movement of the air must be continuous, not a series of jerks. The movement in pitch, too, must go above and below the straight note. Do not at this stage assist the vibrato in any way with the throat, lips, arms, or shoulders. Keep still. Persevere with this exercise until it can be done with ease. This may take a few days or a few minutes; do not proceed until you can do this easily. Now play the scale of G, pulsing eight times on each note. Choose a tempo which suits you then try after a time to increase to ♩=90. Don't let the width of the vibrato get narrower in the middle and upper registers.

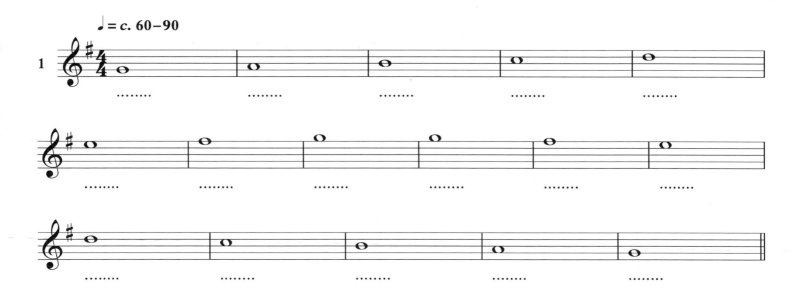

Often the vibrato stops as the note changes. Try to overcome this. Now repeat with six pulses on each note.

Two or three separate ten-minute sessions on these exercises per day will soon produce results. Don't go on until the previous exercise becomes easy. *Time, patience* and *intelligent work.* Now gradually increase the speed, adding slurs: three wobbles per crotchet (or quarter-note).

Be patient: some may find it more difficult than others. Next, find some tunes (hymn tunes are ideal) in which there are no dotted notes, relatively fast-moving notes, or large leaps, for example:

Count four pulses (or even six if played very slowly) on each note. Practise several times each day.
Now for a tune with small leaps. Keep the vibrato moving during the quavers (or eighth-notes):

Don't stop the vibrato between notes. Here is another:

PRAISE TO THE HOLIEST IN THE HEIGHT

Adapted from T. HAWEIS, 1734-1820, by S. WEBBE

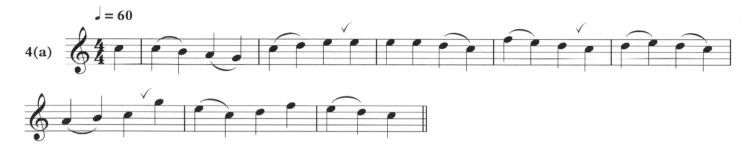

It is a little more difficult to produce the vibrato in the upper register; practise this one carefully. Keep the vibrato going during the shorter notes:

LET US, WITH A GLADSOME MIND

Melody from Hymn tunes of the United Brethren, 1824

The minimum time to have spent on the above and previous exercises would be about three weeks; some will find a longer time is necessary.

STAGE TWO

Vibrato should not be mechanical and calculated. To progress from Stage One to Stage Two involves trying to help the vibrato be *part of the tone* and not something added to it. It is a common problem at this point to choose the speed of the notes to suit the speed of the vibrato. In other words you will find your fingers moving after every fourth or sixth wobble even if the piece is slightly unrhythmic as a result.

How to overcome this:
Play one of the tunes in this way: play the first note without counting the pulses of vibrato and slur on to the next note unpredictably. Some will find this easy, others may not. Then play through the tune using much vibrato but changing notes without reference to the pulses of vibrato.

Play through your tunes using five pulses to each beat, and during the piece, if you happen to use four or six, well, it doesn't matter, does it?

The whole idea of these two ways is to allow the vibrato to be free of the rhythm of the notes so that – like *forte* and *piano* – it can become another cosmetic in your musical make-up bag, to be used in the service of music making.

At this stage you may have observed that the abdominal muscles are causing the larynx or throat to pulse in sympathy. This is fine, but don't assist this throat movement by any sort of tension. Just let it happen. Slowly the larynx will take over a large part of the work. Any forcing of the throat at this point will result in what in the 18th century was called *chevrotement* or a bleating goat vibrato. Save that for your old age!

STAGE THREE

(a) Play this exercise. Use vibrato *through* each note. Keep the vibrato moving all the time:

(b) Choose other tunes with dotted notes, and various other note lengths, but not fast tunes. Be sure the vibrato is ever present, particularly on the long notes. For example:

GOD THAT MADEST EARTH AND HEAVEN
Traditional Welsh

You are over the worst; hereafter it's just practice. You may feel that the vibrato sounds mechanical but your listeners will soon dispel these doubts. This mechanical feeling will soon vanish and vibrato will become part of your tone.

FINAL STAGE

Play the scale of G again:

Without your doing anything to assist it, from G to C the vibrato becomes increasingly wider and, on changing to D, narrower again. It is more difficult to use a wide vibrato when the tube is long. Therefore, practise slow scales to try to maintain the same *pitch change in the vibrato* throughout the scale.

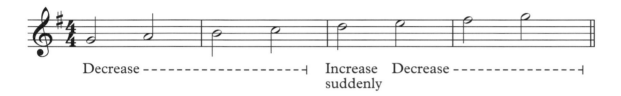

Try other scales as well.

Practise slow scales now throughout the entire compass. The top register may prove to be more difficult and special attention to this register is necessary.

Practise the vibrato at up to and including seven wobbles *per second*. It may begin to even out at six per second until there is an almost straight note. Practice of the earlier exercises, with a wider pitch change will first be necessary. Gradually increase the speed of the wobbles per second. A metronome is indispensable for this.

Vibrato should be present but perhaps to a less noticeable degree in moderately moving quavers (or eighth-notes) at the rate of roughly four per second, otherwise the vibrato sticks out as only being used on long notes. Therefore practise this next exercise first very slowly, with a noticeable vibrato, and increase the speed of the rhythm *without stopping the vibrato* until ♩ = c.132 (see next page).

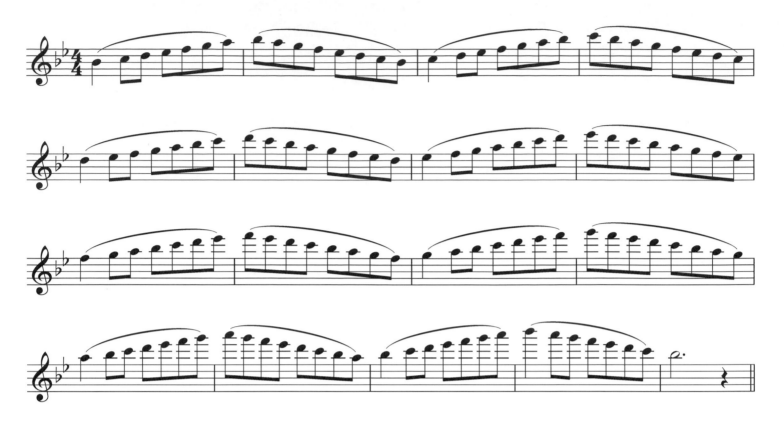

At this point it can almost be said that the wobble has disappeared and in its place is a new-found means of expression. The rest is up to you.

PROBLEMS BOX

1. Vibrato should be within and inside the tone, not added on top. If your tone is small, the vibrato should remain within it. Don't transplant the heart of an elephant into a mouse!

2. If your vibrato was achieved naturally and without thinking about it – lucky you. You shouldn't be reading this box because you have no problems! You may however like to join in at any of the stages to improve your vibrato.

3. If your vibrato sounds like a goat:

   B-aaaaa!

   spend a week or two playing long straight notes, at the end of which start Stage One. In all probability, your throat is tense.

4. Watch yourself in a mirror whilst practising. Are your lips moving? Shoulders? Arms? They shouldn't be.

5. A note should start with vibrato. Many pop and folk singers start a note straight, then add vibrato: this makes the performance gimmicky. Avoid it.

FINALLY

When should vibrato be learned? When the tone has been reasonably developed, though it should not be learned simply to paint over obvious flaws. Most young players seem to adjust easily to learning vibrato after two or three years learning the flute, some even sooner.

Experiment with your new-found expression. Slow, low register tunes may sound best with a gently languid vibrato: exciting tunes, especially in the middle and high register may sound better with a faster vibrato.

Occasionally play an 18th century sonata without vibrato. You may well be called upon to do that in an orchestra some day. It is important to be able to play with little or no vibrato on occasions. 'The Dance of the Blessed Spirits' (*Orfeo* – Gluck), a pure, ethereal, gentle melody, can sound beautiful in this way. It too often sounds like the hip-swinging dance of a chorus girl.

Flute playing is always on the move; changes in style and tone are more obvious examples of changing taste. In the next fifty years one of the changes that must surely come is the control and damping down of vibrato. Its over-use today, especially in the performance of 18th and 19th century music, is most apparent in many orchestras where the flutes can often be heard bleating above the throng.

24 STUDIES FOR INTONATION

Of course, any exercise, played slowly, can become a study for intonation. These short exercises, one in each key, have used the most common intervals to help you develop a keen 'ear'. They are in order of key but not in order of difficulty; you will decide for yourself which are the most difficult. Pay particular attention – even with a 'tuned' flute – to the left hand C♯s and C naturals, and to the lowest notes. Most of the exercises should be repeated an octave higher where a different set of problems will arise. *Avoid playing sharp in the top register*. Practise these studies both *piano* and *forte*, and always slowly.

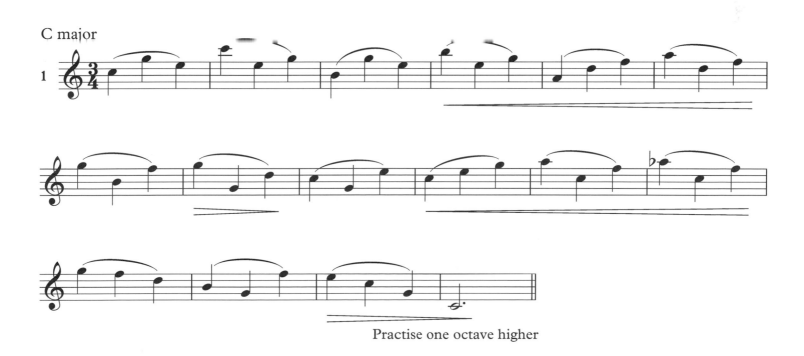

Practise one octave higher

A minor

Practise one octave higher

G major

Practise one octave higher

E minor

cresc.

cresc.

Practise one octave higher

D major

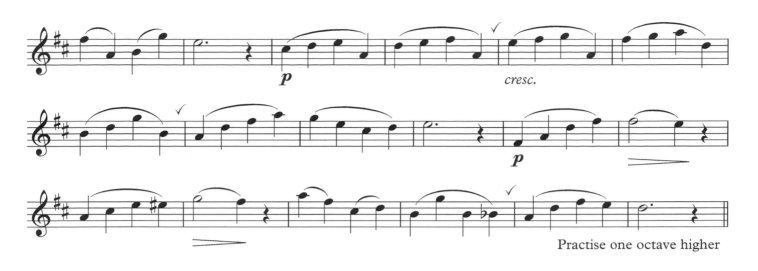

Practise one octave higher

B minor

Practise one octave higher

A major

Practise one octave higher

F♯ minor

Practise one octave higher

E major

Practise one octave higher

C♯ minor

Practise one octave higher

B major

28

Practise one octave higher

G# minor

Practise one octave higher

F# major

Practise one octave higher

E♭ minor

Practise one octave higher

B♭ minor

Practise one octave higher

D♭ major

Practise one octave higher

F minor

Practise one octave higher

A♭ major

30

Practise one octave higher

C minor

19

cresc.

Practise one octave higher

E♭ major

20

cresc.

Practise one octave higher

G minor

21

cresc.

Practise one octave higher

B♭ major

Practise one octave higher

F major

cresc.

cresc.

Practise one octave higher

D minor

cresc.

cresc.

Practise one octave higher

EXAMPLES OF INTONATION PROBLEMS IN MUSICAL WORKS

For the advanced player, the fingering chart as found in beginners books is no longer relevant.

There are many special fingerings which resolve some of the problems of intonation. *The 'correct' fingering is the one that is most in tune.*

Here are some examples of possible – or should I say probable! – intonation problems in the orchestral repertoire. Study of these scores in the light of what has been learned will ease many of the difficulties. I am indebted to Messrs Roger Rostron and Colin Chambers for assistance in compiling this list.

Top of the list: **Mendelssohn's** *Midsummer Night's Dream Overture.*

2) **Rimsky-Korsakov**
   (a) *Scheherazade* – see also bars 314-320, 362-376, 394-401. 1st movement, bar 8 (similar to above). Bars 228 to end in E Major.
   (b) Triplet figure at bar 102 (D).
   (c) 4th movement, bar 655 to the end. The harmonics from 1st desk of violins add problems.

3) **Ravel**
   Bolero – two piccolo variations.

4) **Shostakovich**
   (a) *Symphony No. 5* – 1st movement, bar after (39) solo with horn.
   (b) *Symphony No. 10* – 1st movement, two piccolos at end of movement.
   (c) 3rd movement, flute and piccolo in octaves.

5) **Tchaikovsky**
   (a) *Nutcracker Suite* – 'Dance de Mirlitons' – bar 4: arpeggio.
   (b) *Symphony No. 5* – 4th movement, beginning with bassoons.

6) **Verdi**

(a) *Force of Destiny Overture* – bars 51-66, tuning with oboe and clarinet.

(b) *Sicilian Vespers Overture* – bars 14-33, tuning with two clarinets and bass clarinet in E Major.

(c) *Requiem* – end of 'Lux Aeterna' *pp* to top B♭.

7) **Beethoven**

(a) *Leonora No. 3 Overture* – bars 1-5, 278-294, 301-315, 352-360.

(b) *Symphony No. 7* – 1st movement, bars 56-67 and until 136.

(c) *Piano Concerto No. 5* (Emperor) – slow movement.

8) **Brahms**

(a) *Symphony No. 1* – 1st movement, bars 1-15.

(b) 3rd movement, bars 150 to end, but especially bar 162.

(c) Many of Brahms' Symphonies have movements which end in restrained chords which need careful adjustment.

9) **Debussy**

La Mer – 3rd movement, six bars after 54: long solo with oboe.

10) **Dvořák**

(a) *Symphony No. 9 (New World)* – 2nd movement figure (1) for six bars.

(b) 4th movement after the solo, a long *diminuendo*.

11) **Mendelssohn**

Hebrides Overture – last three bars.

12) **Mozart**

Piano Concertos – the late ones have prominent wind parts. When the piano has not been tuned to A=440, it can play havoc with the woodwind, particularly the clarinets and bassoons which in turn create more problems for the poor flute player.

13) **Wagner**

Tannhäuser Overture – bars 82-94 and 184-190: there is a tendency to get sharp with *crescendo*.

TREVOR WYE

Trevor Wye studied the flute privately both with Geoffrey Gilbert and the celebrated Marcel Moyse. He was a freelance orchestral and chamber music player on the London scene for many years and has made several solo recordings. He was formerly a Professor at the Guildhall School of Music, London and for 21 years at the Royal Northern College of Music in Manchester.

Trevor is the author of the famous *Practice Books* for the flute, which have received worldwide acclaim and have been translated into eleven other languages. More recently, his highly praised biography of Marcel Moyse was published in English and four other languages.

During the year, he teaches at his Flute Studio in Kent, a unique residential course for postgraduate students, and travels throughout the world giving concerts and master classes including annual appearances in the USA, Canada, Europe, Taiwan and Japan and enjoys serving on juries for international competitions.

In 1990 he was made an honorary Fellow of the Royal Northern College of Music by the Duchess of Kent.

TREVOR WYE

Publications by Novello

TUTORS

Beginners Practice Book for the Flute	NOV120848
Proper Flute Playing	NOV120651
Flute Class	NOV121473
Flute Class Concert Album	NOV120784
Practice Book For The Piccolo	NOV120658
The Orchestral Practice Books 1 & 2	NOV120801/NOV120802
The Alto Flute Practice Book	NOV120781
The Complete Daily Exercises	NOV120850
Very First Flute Book	NOV120783

FLUTE & PIANO

A Couperin Album	NOV120609
A Vivaldi Album	NOV120603
A Very Easy Flute Treasury	NOV120852
A First Latin American Flute Album	NOV120634
An Elgar Flute Album	NOV120553
A Schumann Flute Album	NOV120562
A Fauré Flute Album	NOV120542
A Satie Flute Album	NOV120554
A Ravel Album	NOV120741
Schubert: Theme & Variations	NOV120672

FLUTE ENSEMBLE

Three Brilliant Showpieces	NOV120685
Bizet: Jeux D'Enfants	NOV120780

VIDEO

Play the Flute: A beginner's guide	NOV640001

NOVELLO CLASSICS Series

Bach	*B minor Suite*	NOV120767
Mozart	*Concerto No. 2. in D / Andante*	NOV120578
Debussy	*Syrinx*	NOV120756